ANOINTED *FOR* THIS

TRACEY HORN

ANOINTED FOR THIS

TRACEY HORN

Copyright @ 2017 by Tracey Horn

All rights reserved. No part of this publication may be reproduced, distributed, or transmitted in any form or by any means, including photocopying, recording, or other electronic or mechanical methods, without the prior written permission of the publisher, except in the case of brief quotations embodied in critical reviews and certain other noncommercial uses permitted by copyright law. For permission requests, write to the publisher, addressed "Attention: Permissions Coordinator," at the address below.

Tracey Horn
Traceyhorn68@gmail.com

Ordering Information:
Quantity sales: Special discounts are available on quantity purchases by corporations, associations, and others. For details, contact the publisher at the address above.

Published by PTConnection Publisher
Designed By Women's CEO Alliance
Printed in the United States of America

contents

Acknowledgements

Introduction

01
"LIVE"
YOU ARE ANOINTED FOR "THIS"

02
"PURPOSE"
YOU ARE ANOINTED FOR THIS

03
"LIFE"
YOU ARE ANOINTED FOR THIS

contents

04
"AFFLICTIONS"
YOU ARE ANOINTED
FOR THIS

05
"SIT AT THE FEET OF JESUS"
YOU ARE ANOINTED
FOR THIS

06
ANOINTED ONE

APPENDIX

ACKNOWLEDGMENTS

To God, the creator and Lord of my Life, thank you for being my God and allowing me to write this book for your glory.

To my wonderful husband, who loves me through every life-changing event and continues to support and pour himself into me willingly, thank you. Paul, you are my Husband, Prophet, Pastor, Teacher, and Friend. I always find it sweet that my high school sweetheart became such a major and important part of my life and destiny.

To our wonderful children, Derrick, Raven, and Erica, thanks for all you have done and continue doing in my life. You are my cheerleaders and some of my greatest critics for the good.

To the love of all of our lives, Tristan and Payton, our wonderful grandchildren.

I'm grateful for the greatest father, James Earl Ison, for your provisions and sacrifices. Thank you for instilling so much in me and always expressing to me that I can do and achieve anything, even when the devil makes me think I can't. Thank you for imparting into myself and my sisters, Gloria and Angela, the importance of doing good and right. You have such wisdom and grace.

God has graced me throughout my life with wonderful and supporting women that were mother figures: Maude Ison, my grandmother; Maxine Ison, my Aunt; Johnnie Mae Grimsley, mother figure; the late Dorothy Bell Horn, my mother-in-law; Mother Odell Jackson, spiritual and prayer warrior; and last, but certainly not least, Bishop Loretta Smith Johnson, the first bishop to ordain me in ministry at the voice of God.

Other key people in my life include: Pastor Alexis Johnson, Reverend Titus Cummings, Reverend Bobbie and Reverend Angie Cox, the late Reverend Albert Charles and Lady Clovia Mixon, Overseer Joel Parrish, Pastor Jonathan Brown, Presiding Elder David Earl and Allie Bell Reddick, Cecelia Stanford along with Bishop Harry L. and Reverend Sherita M. Seawright, and last and but not least, my Hines Chapel A.M.E. Church family. To God Be the Glory. I am truly blessed and grateful for you all.

Special thanks to Aprill Jones, Tiana Patrice, Tasha Williams and Tyesha Thomas for assisting in making this God-Given Vision come to pass. May God continue to bless and keep you in every endeavor in life.

Introduction

Dear Anointed One,

It is my sincere desire and hope that as you are reading this book, you find yourself in a place of affirmation that no matter what you experience in life, you understand, "You are Anointed for This"! You are anointed to handle every season of your life. You are anointed to handle life because God has equipped you with everything you need to handle it. As a believer, you have been so richly blessed with the anointing of the Holy Spirit that every life event, question, or problem has a solution, God!

I am so excited for you and your future because God's plan for your life causes you to have victory. He has already caused you to live in the richness and abundance of His grace, mercy, and anointing. So, whatever you experience in life, whether it be trials or tribulations, know that you can handle it. Why? Because "You are Anointed for This!"

There may be a ministry that God has inside of you. Do not be afraid. "You are Anointed for This!" My deepest desire is for you to understand that God is with you and will lead you to the destined place He has for you. There may be times where you will have to go down a path of adversities, afflictions, brokenness, or even loneliness. Understand that God's purpose is still within you and He gives you the ability to sit at the feet of Jesus with the Anointing of God on your life.

I wrote this book because it saddens me to see so many Christians proclaim the Word of God, but live defeated lives. I know what it feels like to feel defeated and cry in the dark. I know what it feels like to have suicidal thoughts with seemingly no way out. Had it not been for the grace of God in my life, I may have tried to escape my circumstances using ways that are not of God. I had to learn and understand that I was anointed for those times, just like YOU are anointed for yours. It is my aspiration that you will be so empowered through reading the pages of this book that your life will be transformed and you will set out to be all God has called you to be.

I wrote this book from a place that some Christians are skeptical to address. Hopeless thoughts. Brokenness. Depression. Any area of your life where challenges, struggles, afflictions, sufferings, or battles reside… so does the anointing of God. "You are Anointed for This!"

The "this" in your life may look different than mine; however, it is the necessary thing that you must go through in order to get to your NEXT in life. The "this" in your life is what will help push you into your purpose and destiny. Every "this" you experience is essential to the process of living a fulfilled life in Christ Jesus. Your "this" is critical and leads you to the manifestation of God's anointing. Do not be afraid of your "this". Do not run from your "this". Embrace it. Trust the process. "You are Anointed for This."

Yours in Christ,
Tracey Horn

01

LIVE

01

LIVE, YOU ARE ANOINTED FOR THIS

As I reflect over my life, I am astonished to see how God directed my path to get me to my purpose. I was born in Newark, New Jersey, then moved to a small town called Shorterville, Alabama. It was all part of God's strategic plan. From there I moved to Lawrenceville, Alabama, then to Eufaula, Alabama, where my life continued to flourish. A Jersey girl, in Alabama! Look at God. He knew exactly what He was doing. God is so amazing in His infinite wisdom! Throughout the years, I learned that he will direct your path in such a way that he will allow situations and disturbances to get you to where you need to be. Even on the darkest paths in life, he will direct your path for good, and not for bad, much like he did with Abram. The Bible states in Genesis 12:1-3 The LORD had said to Abram, *"Go from your country, your people and your father's household to the land I will show you. ² I will make you into a great nation, and I will bless you; I will make your name great, and you will be a blessing. ³ I will bless those who bless you, and whoever curses you I will curse; and all peoples on earth will be blessed through you."* So Abram went, as the LORD had told him. You see, sometimes the assignment is unusual, but it's necessary for your elevation and new position.

When purpose and destiny calls, your next response is critical.

It was time for Abram to move into his anointed place, Father of Nations. God did not tell Abram where he was going, Abram just listened to the voice of God and God manifested every promise unto him. Making critical moves aren't always easy. I remember making a critical move in my life to go back to school. My circumstances said no, but God said yes. My husband and I had one child, and going back to school would require a lot of my time. Our finances would be cut a great deal, as I would need to take a different job that would allow me the time I needed to go to school. However, I kept hearing the Holy Spirit tell me to go back to school! After discussing it more with my husband, we decided it was best for me to go in the direction that I was being led. This meant sacrifices would have to be made. I took a lesser paying job to pursue going to college. I worked during the day and went to school full-time at night. It was an absolute a walk of faith. However, when I finished school, God allowed me to receive a job that almost tripled my previous salary with great benefits. You see, the road isn't always going to be easy, but it's so necessary for your NEXT.

Sometimes you just have to step out on faith and do what God says, even when the odds seem against you. "You are Anointed for This!" Obedience is the difference between being blessed or cursed, having abundance or lacking, or life and death.

Your obedience to God causes you to live a blessed life. God, being all-knowing, knows the direction you should take. He will order your steps, while your role is only to be obedient to his leading. Sometimes God's direction for your life may be questionable to you, but it's critical that you follow Him and move at His command. God can see much further than you can. He knows your beginning and your end. He will not lead you wrong. Every word He speaks is dependable and reliable because He cannot lie. God is trustworthy and has your best interest at all times.

"You are Anointed for This!" You have to trust God and be obedient to His voice as well as step out on faith. You see, faith gets God's attention so much that He will cause heaven and earth to move to bless you. There are times in life that you have to believe God for what your eyes can't see. What would have happened if I had chosen not to walk in faith and trust God? Honestly, I don't want to know. I may have never reached the place or position I am in, that's for sure.

As I continued to walk in faith and obedience, God opened up Heaven again just for me. He took me from being a Sunday school teacher, to teaching in a women's ministry through "Women Walking with Purpose," and then to preaching and proclaiming God's Word in the Ordained Ministry of the African Methodist Episcopal Denomination.

When I think about the goodness of God and His thoughts towards me, tears begin to fall down my face. I understand, God was working things out for my good, even when it didn't look like it or feel like it. Even when the world didn't understand and criticized me, God had already worked out the perfect plan for my life.

He reminded me that I was indeed Anointed for This!

Throughout life, Romans 8:28 continues to prove true in my life. Not just my life, but the lives of all born-again believers. Romans 8:28 says *"And we know that all things work together for good to them that love God, to them who are the called according to his purpose."* All things work together for them that love God! Therefore, you must believe through difficult times, it's working! Transitional times, it's working! Through trials and tribulations, it's working! God is preparing you for your anointed places. "You are Anointed for This!"

02

PURPOSE

02

Purpose, You Are Anointed for This

Have you ever been in a place where it appears everything and everyone you thought was part of your purpose seems to have drifted away? The things you thought you wanted seem to no longer make you feel that you are significant, purposed or anointed. This means you are in the middle of a shift.

The plan God has for your life requires you to have the ability to shift. The plan God has for your life will never change, however, the direction and course of your life may. This means God is beginning to maneuver you through his perfect plan to lead you into your purpose and destiny. Psalms 37:23 reminds us that "*The steps of a good man are ordered by the Lord: and he delighteth in his way.*" Believers must buy-in to the ordering system of God to operate in the plan of God for their life.

Jeremiah 29:11 helps us to understand why buy-in is critical. God's ways and thoughts are so much greater than ours. We simply have to trust his plan and move in the direction He leads. After experiencing challenges with certain relationships in my life, the enemy began combatting my thoughts about purpose in those relationships. I realized I had made others the entire purpose of my existence. I had stumbled into a place of complacency and was comfortable in the circles I was in. Complacency is never a position to be in when dealing with the Will of God for your life. Complacency puts you in a stagnant place where you can't receive change, even when change is knocking at your door. Change is inevitable when submitting to the Will of God. If everybody did the same things, followed the same routines, talked to the same people, went to the same places, the Gospel of Christ would not spread throughout the world and the great commission would not be fulfilled. This means you may need to change some things, change some circles, change some relationships, to be fully entered into God's perfect plan for your life.

Change can be accepted willingly, or God has a way of changing circumstances and situations to cause you to shift. God's plan for your life will call for a shift, moving you from purpose to purpose into your divine, destined place. Being able to shift and move in a different direction and focus is crucial even when dealing with those you are closest to, such as your spouse and children. It is imperative to understand that they have purpose just like you. Their dependency and reliability will have to shift towards their God given purpose, and so should yours. You cannot be an effective vessel of God and not embrace versatility, change and transition.

Purpose isn't easy. I was reminded of this after receiving altered instructions in my teaching career. I remember having to change grade levels after teaching Kindergarten for three years. I was so upset because I thought Kindergarten was part of my purpose, but the truth is, I had become complacent instead of leaning on the Lord. As I was walking down the first grade hall, The Spirit spoke to me so clearly saying, "Do not get comfortable because your life is not a life of comfort." While I didn't understand the fullness of that message, I accepted the will of God and moved into my new season. As the word would have it, I later understood that revelation when I was moved again from being a classroom teacher to being an administrator of an elementary school. After the physical shift happened, then the spiritual shift happened, from ministry leadership to preaching and proclaiming the Word of God. Shifts happen to move us from one place to another and from one position to the next. These changes in my life would not have occurred if I had not trusted the shifting of God. I could have fought for what I thought was my position. I could have said no. But when purpose and destiny knock at your door, you don't say no…you say, "Hello!" "You are anointed for This!"

Don't get caught up on thinking purpose will always be the same; there is a constant shifting in the life of the Anointed! If you are battling with major shifts in purpose and life, understand you are a prime candidate for use by the Master, and you may even be a carrier of the anointing of God! Sometimes God's plan requires a stretching or expansion of mind because He knows every detail of your life and the great work He desires to accomplish through you! You are needed for such a time as this. Just like the Book of Esther. Because she was able to shift and allow God to change the direction of her purpose, she was able to change the destiny of her people. God wants to use you in a mighty way, but you must be available and allow the anointing in your life to transition and shift you; however, and whenever God directs the shifting. Just know, you may not only be anointed to change your life or your family's life, but a whole nation. Purpose will cause you to walk away from people and things that aren't in alignment with your purpose. Purpose will cause you to go to foreign lands you are neither comfortable nor familiar with, in order to lead you to your destiny. You are anointed for your purpose!

After going through life experiences and circumstances where the very people and things I valued and poured my whole life into didn't appear to have the same outlook, I was forced to remember the promises of God and the things and people God called me to. The enemy will attempt to make you feel that you are insignificant and not valued if you allow him to. James 4:7 tells us to *"Submit yourselves therefore to God. Resist the devil, and he will flee from you."* The season of purpose you are in leaves no room for the enemy to clog your thoughts with negative and false ideas. The truth of the matter is, you are indeed needed and valued by God for the intended season of purpose He has you in. Purpose is knocking at your door. Will you answer?

Never forget you are anointed for purpose and destiny.

A Prayer for Purpose

Father God in Heaven, You know me better than I know myself. Lord, I desire to live out an abundant life with purpose, but I have been struggling to embrace it. I believe your Holy promise in John 10:10. It assures me that this kind of living is possible. However, I need your help. I give you my fears with every known and unknown reservation within me. I trust you Lord and I am certain you can set me free. Lord, let your will be released in me. Thank you for anointing me to Live an abundant life with purpose. In Jesus name I pray, Amen!

By: Tyeshia Thomas

List Every Obstacle that Keeps You from Your God-Given Purpose Below:

_____
_____
_____
_____
_____
_____
_____
_____
_____
_____
_____
_____
_____
_____
_____

NOW, SURRENDER THEM ALL TO GOD!

03

LIFE

03

LIFE, YOU ARE ANOINTED FOR THIS

Family is one of the strongest links that holds the weakest links together in life, because family is the second order of God. After the creation of the heavens and earth, God created man. God decided it was not good for man to be alone, and as a result, woman was pulled from the side of man and created by the hand of God. God gave them specific instructions in Genesis 1:28 *"And God blessed them, and God said unto them, Be fruitful, and multiply, and replenish the earth, and subdue it: and have dominion over the fish of the sea, and over the fowl of the air, and over every living thing that moveth upon the earth."*

Being fruitful is bearing and giving birth. This order was established from the beginning of man's existence, thus exemplifying God first, man next, then woman as man's helper and children. Because this is the order of God, the enemy comes in any way he can to cause disorder to what God has ordered.

It is the enemy's job and goal to dismantle the family. If he can dismantle the family, nothing else can grow, flow, nor develop because of the broken link of family. John 10:10 helps in understanding *"The thief cometh not, but for to steal, and to kill, and to destroy: I am come that they might have life, and that they might have it more abundantly."* Isaiah 59:19 tells us *"So shall they fear the name of the Lord from the west, and his glory from the rising of the sun. When the enemy shall come in like a flood, the Spirit of the Lord shall lift up a standard against him."* Yes, the enemy will come in and try to dishonor what God has honored, family, but You are Anointed for This.

There are times when it feels that life has the best of you. Feelings of loneliness and being unloved by those you love the most can be overwhelming. You must always understand, as a child of God, that you are never alone and always loved. God will never leave you nor forsake you. Understanding who you are and to whom you belong will be your greatest weapon against the enemy during difficult times in life. The enemy is not only after your mind, he is after your peace, love, joy and happiness. It goes even deeper than that. He is not just after you and your family, he is also after your Anointing. He understands if the link is broken, the family will not exist properly and there will be a hindrance to the building of God's Kingdom. Thanks be to God that cares for us! He has given us power to withstand all attacks on the family. "You are Anointed for This!"

Knowing the power of God through His Word, prayer, and meditation on the importance of God's covenant will help you to understand the bond that cannot be broken by the fiery darts of the enemy. Your confession must be, "I am loved, nurtured, and cared for by God." He cares for you more than you can even imagine. His very thoughts are of you. His plan is to bring you to a prosperous and expected end. He knows your beginning and your end. His love goes deeper than any valley and wider than any mountain.

There isn't anything God will not do for you when you honor and keep his covenant and understand you are anointed to handle obstacles. Trust is your foundation during extreme times like these. Trust in the Lord with your whole heart and lean not to your own understanding, acknowledge Him and He will direct your path. These emotional distractions could be a setup to draw you closer to God and to understand joy, contentment, peace and the love that comes only from God. God may be trying to draw you closer to him and build that intimate relationship that he desires to have with you.

I fell prey to the emotional roller coaster of the enemy by subjecting myself to feeling alone and unloved. Growing up in a single parent home, while my father was amazing, there were things that I didn't understand how to handle when I became an adult. After I fell in love and married my awesome husband, issues surfaced that I expected him to fix. While Paul continued to love me and care for me, the reality was that he could never fix me. God is the only one that can change hearts, minds, and souls. God wants your expectations to be on him, not on man. Man is not perfect, but God is.

There was a powerful lesson there for me to learn. I had to build a relationship with God for myself through meditating on the Word of God, fasting and praying, and going into a deeper level of praise and worship. I had to experience His love for myself. The more I surrendered to God, the more He began showing me who I am. There was a love beyond man's love, and I finally began to experience that love! While my husband loved me, he could never be my God. There is only one true and living God, and He is irreplaceable.

The sooner I understood that, the more God revealed to me more and more of Him.

God is the only one who can make all things new. God is a strong tower, deliverer, healer, and conqueror. Because He lives, we are more than conquerors through Christ Jesus who strengthens us. I'll be honest, I didn't realize that the anointing of God on my life was much stronger than my circumstances. I had to learn that there is nothing too hard for God, and he is able, willing and committed to keep us from falling.

You are anointed to handle life situations and circumstances through the power of the Holy Spirit. There is no situation too big for God. There is no circumstance that He cannot fix. There are no setbacks that the Almighty power of God has not already set you up for victory and deliverance. You are anointed to stand, anointed to succeed, anointed to survive, and anointed to conquer all. Romans 8:37 encourages us to know that *"Nay, in all these things we are more than conquerors through him that loved us."*

Sometimes the enemy tries to make you feel insignificant and like you don't matter. This is the biggest lie from the enemy. God has fearfully and wonderfully created you to be who you are. Love yourself and know that God loves you. God loves you so much that he sent His Son Jesus, through 42 generations, to live and die for your sins. Yes, He died just for you. But we all know, that's not the end of the story. Jesus rose with all power so that you can live an abundant life. Know that He has given you qualities and characteristics that look like him and sound like Him. No weapon formed against you shall ever prosper. They will form, however, the anointing and power of God will not allow them to prosper. All things have been crafted and designed to work together for them that love God and are called according to His purpose. "You are Anointed for This!" You have the Almighty God on your side.

One of our greatest fears is when the family is compromised. There was a time in my life when my marriage was under attack. I found myself in a place of compromise. What if my marriage ends up in divorce? What would I do? What is going to happen to me and our children? I remember feeling down one Saturday morning, stuck in my emotions, when a very dear friend to my husband and I, Overseer Joel Parrish called me to come over to his house for prayer. I will never forget the day. He, along with two other prayer warriors, prayed for me and my husband. They were standing in the gap praying, rebuking the enemy and declaring the success of my marriage. In that very hour, my heart and perspective about my marriage changed.

After that prayer meeting, the option of divorce was no longer a thought in my mind. Praying, meditating on the Word of God, praising God and worshipping God became my life. I knew my marriage was the will of God and I wasn't going to let fear control the outcome of my marriage. God has a way of drawing you closer to him during the processes of life that try to push you away. It was through this experience, that I drew closer to God and my worship grew deeper with God. I often tell people, I thank God for that experience because it took my praise and worship to another dimension that deepened my relationship with God and simultaneously strengthened my marriage. Now, the God I knew to be a comforter, restorer, deliver and friend, also restored and delivered our marriage. God put us together and our destiny was not going to be altered because of the devices of the enemy. Whom God put together, no man shall separate. I learned a valuable life lesson; it is in the winter seasons of life God will show you a different perspective of who He is. God is faithful, and His Word is true. He will be whatever you need Him to be, and You are Anointed for This.

PRAYER TO LIVE LIFE ABUNDANTLY

Gracious God in Heaven, thank you for abundant life, good health and strength. Thank you for marriage, children, grandchildren, family and everyone else connected to me. Lord, thank you for being our source of abundant living. Thank you for placing the power to get wealth inside of us. Thank you for ensuring that as children of God we can prosper according to 3 John 1:2 which states, *"Beloved, I wish above all things that thou mayest prosper and be in health, even as thy soul prospereth."* Thank you for confirming your promise that we are healed by the stripes of Jesus in Isaiah 53:5. Thank you allowing our marriages to be abundantly blessed and secured in you. Thank you for my children being blessed to live abundant lives. Thank you for financial stability.

Thank you for every opportunity to receive the abundance of Heaven. Thank you for being the sole provider of all our needs. Thank you for satisfying our desires according to your word in Psalm 145:16 which states, *"Thou openest thine hand, and satisfiest the desire of every living thing."* Lord God, thank you for commanding plenteous blessing and favor to fall upon us. Thank you for your bountiful peace covering us. We come seeking you with expectations that we will lack no good thing. Thank you for total life prosperity, abundance of power, courage to embrace the fullness of joy, and strength. Thank you for teaching us how to abound in love and how to exemplify unwavering faith. Thank you for granting us a fulfilled life. Thank you for opening the way for us to live an abundant life in you. We gratefully embrace this opportunity. Heavenly Father, let your will be done. In Jesus name we pray, Amen!

By: Tyeshia Thomas

List Every Obstacle that Keeps You from Living an Abundant Life Below:

_____
_____
_____
_____
_____

NOW, SURRENDER THEM ALL TO GOD!

04

AFFLICTIONS

04

Afflictions, You Are Anointed for This

Afflictions are characterized as a state of pain, distress, grief or misery, or a cause of mental or bodily pain, as sickness, loss or persecution. You may be experiencing afflictions in your life that cause you much pain. When afflictions come, you must resort to what the Word of God has to say about the matter. Psalm 34:19 says *"Many are the afflictions of the righteous: but the LORD DELIVERETH HIM OUT OF THEM ALL."* Whatever your affliction may be, know and believe that God has the power and authority to deliver you. Isaiah 53:5 says *"But he was wounded for our transgressions, he was bruised for our iniquities: the chastisement of our peace was upon him; and with his stripes we are healed."*

One of the most difficult times in my life was in 2013. After having numerous painful headaches and problems with my vision, I was diagnosed with multiple sclerosis. Before I was diagnosed, I started taking medication for what I thought was a bad sinus infection. The medicine never worked. I finally went to my family physician, who sent me to the eye doctor. After not getting any results, I was referred to an ear, nose, and throat specialist. After hours and more tests, the doctor sent me to another eye specialist. This specialist immediately recognized something else was going on and it had nothing to do with needing glasses or minor eye complications. He immediately called and rushed me through the process of having an MRI. The next morning, I was being referred to a neurologist. After several tests, the doctor suspected that multiple sclerosis was going to be the diagnosis. He sent me to the local hospital to have a spinal tap and from that test, he confirmed his suspicion of multiple sclerosis. My husband and I went to a specialist 4 hours away for a second opinion only to be hit with the same diagnosis. We didn't understand anything about this condition, but was told by everyone that it was a lifelong process. Daily injections, multiple pills, and self-sabotaging thoughts became my daily routine. I began having pity parties and waddled in doubt. While my family was very supportive and we continued to stand on faith, I couldn't help but think about life and the ups and downs I had experienced. I began crying wondering if life would somehow be different if I was someone else! Struggling to physically see with limited and blurred vision, I had to come to a decision in my life. Will this be life or death? I could not stop thinking about the promises for my life. God had promised me some things, and this was not a part of the promises he made to me. I stopped doubting God and began putting my mind and thoughts on His promises and prophecies over my life. I began focusing on what He had shown me in the Spirit, and what He showed me did not look like my current status.

You must understand and build such a relationship with God, that you know when afflictions come, God is up to something good! You must get an expectation and become joyful because God chose you to give permission for Satan to touch. God allows some things to happen because he has an investment in you and is waiting for a return. There must be a constant reminding that God never permits anything to happen for our harm. The result will ALWAYS be victory! Knowing the promises God made to me caused my faith to increase! There was a determination that I could not give up on all my hopes, dreams and promises because God had something for me to do. I began walking around in our quiet, still home praying about my situation and reminding God that I was waiting for the things he promised to manifest because I believed it to be so. The spirit reminded me that God is a promise keeper, and the plan He has for my life was a great and successful plan! The Holy Spirit brought back to my remembrance how God delivered me in the past. He reminded me of the season I entered in where I was afflicted with a bulging disk. In this season I was unable to walk without a walker or a cane, and was unsure if I was ever going to walk again. In the midst of it all, I trusted God that my current state would not be my ending state. And guess what? God healed me, and I received the activity of my limbs again to walk. My expectation every morning became an anticipation of the deliverance from God. I woke up with the expectation and anticipation, asking God Questions. "Is this the day you are going to deliver me? Is this the day you are going to do for me what I couldn't do for myself?" My complaint became such a reverence for God until I understood that God was not going to leave me in that condition, because He still had work for me to do!

My story reminds me of the story in the Bible about the woman with the issue of blood that had gone from doctor to doctor. She spent all she had, and her issue was still her issue. She had an issue of blood for many years. She tried natural means, but it took the supernatural measures and faith to receive what she wanted from God. She heard Jesus was coming through her city, and hope arose within her. *If I can just touch the hem of Jesus' garment, I will be made whole.* She pressed her way through the crowd, touched the garment of Jesus, and he not only healed her, but made her whole. I began pressing and reading different stories in the bible where God did it for his people. I remember walking into my bedroom and heard the voice of the Lord say, "I shall get glory out of this." I remember thinking, "Glory? But God, I can't see! Glory? God, I can't even proclaim the Word of God! Glory? God, how am I going to travel and minister to your people that you have called me to without vision?" But here's the thing, the enemy always wants to shift our focus from the possibilities of God to focus on the restraints of him.

Remember, if there are restrictions, it's not God. If the enemy is trying to put chains on you, bind you up, afflict you, and attach diseases and illnesses to your name, it's not God's will for you. Jesus suffered, died and was raised from the dead that you may have life and life more abundantly. As I began focusing on what God had to say about the matter verses the diagnosis of man, impossibilities became possibilities, sickness became healing, shackles were loosed, and the spirit of bondage no longer had a hold on me. I learned no matter what is taking place in life, if I just keep my eyes on the Master, everything else will be alright.

Whatever your current state is, whether it be pain, sickness, disease, bondage of sin, just know what you say and speak out of your mouth will determine your outcome. You must speak life and not death. Proverbs 18:21 helps us to understand and believe that *"Death and life are in the power of the tongue: and they that love it shall eat the fruit thereof."* When I started looking to God and not my situation, I immediately began experiencing God in a greater way in my life. Something began to happen on the inside of me that pushed me to a different level in God and a different level of faith. The anointing began pulling on me and caused a shift in my situation as I began praying.

There was a sudden shift in my spirit. God was not finished with me yet! His purpose and destiny was not complete; therefore, my current state could not possibly be my end state. Hope arose within. That healing had to take place! In prayer time, I would remind God of who He is: a provider, deliverer, healer, promise keeper and that He wasn't a liar! In this season, I was given a book, and it changed my life forever. In the book, a woman had been diagnosed with multiple sclerosis. She gave her account of the process she went through before God healed her. Revelation revealed that her faith had to be shifted to another dimension. This helped me to understand that healing is activated by faith in the Word of God, and faith is a mindset that comes from the heart. I began reading passages of scriptures and stories in the Bible of God healing people. How He healed the woman with the issue of blood, the healing of the lame man, the blind man receiving sight, Lazarus being raised from the dead, and so many more biblical references infused my spirit. I began believing God for my healing. I understood that God has no respect of persons. I believe to this day that I'm healed, and my healing was complete by the stripes Jesus unjustly endured on the cross. Isaiah 53:5 states *"But He was wounded for our transgressions, He was bruised for our iniquities; The chastisement for our peace was upon Him, And by His stripes we are healed."* No matter what life circumstances and situations brings your way, remember who God is. He is a healer, deliverer and a miracle worker.

Life experiences were helping me understand I was anointed for this! Any situation and circumstance that arises in the lives of God's people, remember you have been anointed to handle and go through every storm and strong wind that may blow in your life! Remember, it won't last always! There is an end. Psalms 34:19 gives us an assurance of healing and deliverance: *"Many are the afflictions of the righteous: but the* Lord delivereth him out of them all.." Every person I read about in the bible that came to Jesus for healing and deliverance were delivered from there infirmities. The ones that did not receive their miracles were those that could not believe Jesus to be a deliverer and healer. Don't you see that you are anointed for this! You were anointed in the womb according to Jeremiah 1:5. I am currently in my yet season! I have not received the doctors report of complete healing yet, but I know that I am healed according to the Word of God, so until the MRI scans confirm and line up with my belief and faith of no lesions, no hurt, harm, nor damage to any part of my body in Jesus' name, I will still rejoice that Christ sealed the deal over two thousand years ago!

A Prayer for Afflictions

Merciful Father in Heaven, your word teaches in Psalm 34:19, *"Many are the afflictions of the righteous: but the LORD DELIVERETH HIM OUT OF THEM ALL."* Lord, I know that afflictions must come, and I am confident that they have a purpose in my life, but I need help keeping my peace intact while enduring afflictions. Lord, your word promises me in Isaiah 26:3, *"Thou wilt keep him in perfect peace, whose mind is stayed on thee: because he trusteth in thee."* Lord, in times of affliction, teach me how to focus more on you and what you promised. Teach me how to express the hope, patience and continuous prayer that I have read about in Romans 12:12. Lord, I come releasing all my anxieties to you. I'm glad that I'm able to run to you and find peace. I'm able to find rest and safety in your presence. I humbly pray that you give me endurance to make it through every affliction without giving up and resilience to bounce back from all pain and suffering. Lord, I love, trust and appreciate you. Thank you for anointing me to handle afflictions. In Jesus' name, Amen!

By: Tyeshia Thomas

List Every Affliction in Your Life Below:

_____
_____
_____
_____
_____
_____
_____
_____

NOW, SURRENDER THEM ALL TO GOD!

05

SIT AT THE FEET OF JESUS

05

SIT AT THE FEET OF JESUS, YOU ARE ANOINTED FOR THIS

An indication of your anointing is when you learn how to sit at the feet of Jesus! There is humility that comes along with the anointing of God. Anointed people understand they can't do anything of themselves, only by the power and authority of God! Sitting at the feet of Jesus means you enter into a place of oneness with Christ Jesus. Nothing else matters. Nothing enters in except you and God. At the feet of Jesus, humility exists. There is no room for pride, arrogance or flesh. At His feet, nothing enters in but truth. God already knows the truth; therefore, you must be willing to enter into a place of worship totally depending on God and acknowledging that He is in total control and nothing matters except what He says. He has the final word and any actions after that are dependent upon what you have learned and heard at His feet. At the feet of Jesus is where you understand it's not about you, but all about God. At His feet is where you discover the very heart of God for your life. You understand your responsibility and duty as a member in the Body of Christ. Everything you do is at the heart of Jesus, so at His feet is where you find the revelation of God for your life! Your next direction is given at his feet. Your next mission is revealed at the Master's feet. Purpose and destiny is made known at his feet. The next move of God is discovered at His feet.

Often, it's when our backs are against the wall and trials and tribulations drive us to our knees, that God prepares us for our next in life. It wasn't until many in the Bible experienced bondage or difficult times that God unveiled another part of His plan for their lives! In the fifth chapter of Mark, the Bible reveals that a man with many evil spirits goes out to meet Jesus and the evil spirits plead with Jesus to leave them alone and not cast them out. God, being a gracious God and purposeful God, delivered the man from torment and set him free! This man sat at the feet of Jesus after his deliverance and requested to follow Jesus, but Jesus gave him his assignment to go back to his family and tell them everything the Lord had done for him and how merciful Jesus had been to him. The man's witness of Jesus was so powerful that the people openly received Jesus and was amazed at what Jesus had done. The man sat at the feet of Jesus long enough to get what he needed to effectively complete the task before him. Remember, the steps of God's anointed are ordered by God! At His feet, He reminds you of His word, His plans, His direction, peace, joy and fulfillment. Often the pressures of life put us at the feet of Jesus, but there are also times, out of relationship with God, the anointed willingly sit at His feet!

There are times when Christians arrive to a place of dependency on God that the feet of Jesus becomes their daily ambition. Nothing makes sense or matters until you reach the feet of Jesus, meaning total dependency is on God, what he has to say and his guidance. My joy is getting in his presence and sitting at His feet. The reliance of life is so detrimental that in the morning before seeking anyone or anything else, God is the first contact- understanding only He has what you need for the day. One's heart is not regulated without him.

There are times when life's battles will make you feel as if you are suffocating and can't breathe. The Spirit of God reminds you that God is the creator of your heart, and He knows the heartbeats and just what it takes to make your heart function properly. God knows the rhythm and has the capability of fixing your heart and controlling the rhythm of your heart. The mind is not conditioned until an encounter has been made with Jesus. The plan for the day is not clear until sitting at His feet. The relationship is built so that the very existence depends totally on God and one's communion with Him first. Walking, talking and living is credited to the feet of God. When one understands the criticalness of sitting at the feet of Jesus, that individual understands who the anointing is dependent on. Life experiences help in understanding life is not life until you learn how to submit to God and sit at His feet.

The disciples sat at the feet of Jesus to be taught during Jesus' earthly ministry. We must be willing to sit at His feet in the Spirit to be taught and partake of the intimacy of God that is only revealed at His feet. For some, trouble draws them to the feet of Jesus. I willingly sit at the feet of Jesus. Not saying I have it all figured out, but I learned a long time ago that sitting at the feet of Jesus is an honor, privilege and profitable. After my husband and I gave our lives to Christ, there was a hunger and thirst for the presence of God. We ran after every experience and opportunity to enter in His presence. We would use our home as a sanctuary for the presence and glory of God. You see, God had shown us a side of Him that was addictive. We would host praise and worship at our house with a couple of friends. I believe our house was a safe dwelling place for God's presence. We would stay after services at church just to get closer to Him. We would visit churches that were experiencing the presence and power of God. As a matter of fact, it was a small Church of God in Christ Church that my husband and I gave our lives to Christ. Not only that, but it was the same revival that Paul proposed to me in service. It was so amazing, and course I said yes. After service, I remember asking Paul did he really mean to propose to me. I had to make sure he was sincere and it just wasn't the Spirit speaking, so I confirmed with Him after service that it was his sincere desire. I often tell people that God made Paul marry me because of the way he proposed to me.

    I remember an anointed gathering at our house when we were experiencing the awesome power of God. Lives were being changed! People were being encouraged, but most of all, God was being glorified. As I worshipped God while kneeling, one of the ladies worshipping God while standing accidentally fell on my foot. I remember as if it was yesterday. Everyone literally heard my ankle crack. We began praying and had a healing service right there in our home. Instantly, I remember Paul laying his hands on my ankle and praying the prayer of healing for my ankle. After prayer, I stood up. There was no pain, nothing out of place nor broken. God had healed my ankle right in my home. Can you imagine the praise and worship that broke out in our home on that glorious night? At the feet of Jesus, God reveals His mighty power to those that believe.

    I urge you not to wait until times are tough to submit yourself to the feet of Jesus, but willingly make it priority, a pleasure and honor to sit there. Don't wait until your marriage is in trouble, your children are acting up, the doctor pronounces a diagnosis, confusion troubles your mind, or the enemy attacks you fiercely to sit at the Master's feet. He will teach you everything you need to know at His feet. Wow, what an awesome God we serve! Your life will never be the same again. He will reveal unmeasurable and untold mysteries through His Word and the Holy Spirit. My daily reverence starts with acknowledgment of who God is and a salutation to the mighty anointing of the Holy Spirit, my comforter, encourager, motivator, director, and friend. I want God to know that I am appreciative to Him as well as the Holy Spirit He sent to seal and keep me. Sit at His feet, "You are Anointed for This."

A Prayer to Sit at His Feet

Heavenly Father, My Daddy in Heaven, I come to you with child-like faith. I come with a deep sense of longing to be taught the depths of your love. Teach me your ways like you taught Mary, the sister of Lazarus. I come presenting you my ears to hear and a deep longing within myself to know you in a deeper way. I come with earnest desire to learn your statures. Take me to that intimate place with you. Expose me to the place in you, where my life, perspectives, attitudes and habits change.

Allow me to experience your peace and joy in a greater unexplainable way. Thank you for this honor and privilege to sit humbly at your feet while you reveal unto me who you created and purposed me to be. Thank you for loving and anointing me to sit at your feet. In Jesus' name, Amen!

By: Tyeshia Thomas

List Every Distraction that Keeps You from the Feet of Jesus Below:

_____
_____
_____
_____
_____
_____
_____
_____

NOW, SURRENDER THEM ALL TO GOD!

06

ANOINTED ONE

06

ANOINTED ONE

Prayerfully, "Anointed for This" has exposed devises and plans of the enemy as well as the mighty power of the Almighty God to change and direct your life to the anointed place God has called you to. His plans are the only things that are important, and the sooner you understand this, the greater the anointing He has placed within you will manifest and be revealed. God wants to get glory out of your life, no matter what you experience. God knows every detail of your life, even the number of hairs on your head. There isn't anything you experience that He doesn't know and care about. This book reveals real life experiences that I have encountered. Some experiences were more challenging than others. My testimony is that He has caused me to win over and through them all. God's grace, mercy, love and anointing for me causes me to continue to win no matter what attacks come my way.

I want you to understand that troubles will come, as they are designed to, but you have an advocate that has already fought for you through every life experience, and the result is constantly the same. You are victorious! God loves you unconditionally. He loves you so much that He will allow obstacles to disturb your life to get you to where you are supposed to be. I often call obstacles, trials, tribulations, afflictions and adversities spiritual bumpers to bump you in the right direction.

God has equipped you with everything you need, for you are an overcomer. Live your best life, trusting God, believing the impossible, overcoming every obstacle and living in the abundance of God through His Word, The Holy Spirit, praise and worship, and sitting at His feet for every direction in life. This may sound super spiritual to some, but this is the only way you can live the fulfilled life God has for you through intimacy and relationship with Him. May the joy of the Lord fill your hearts and souls! Blessings and Peace!

APPENDIX

Appendixes of Weapons and Scriptures to Combat Attacks of the Enemy

Appendix A:
The Anointing and Power of God's Word

The Anointed study the Word of God because it is daily bread. The Bible also lets us know that study, meditation and application of the Word of God is critical in the lives of believers. The only way we can know, understand and gain access to the promises of God is through His divine Word. We are to study to show ourselves approved. Application of the Word on a continuous basis builds your faith and gives the Holy Spirit something to pull up at the point of need. My weapon and defense against every attack of the enemy in my life is the Word of God. It is the Word of God that cuts down, breaks up, and ultimately destroys the plans and devices of the devil. These powerful scriptures help in understanding the anointing and power in the Word of God.

Hebrews 4:12 - For the word of God [is] quick, and powerful, and sharper than any two-edged sword, piercing even to the dividing asunder of soul and spirit, and of the joints and marrow, and [is] a discerner of the thoughts and intents of the heart.

Jeremiah 23:29 - [Is] not my word like as a fire? saith the LORD; and like a hammer [that] breaketh the rock in pieces?

2 Timothy 3:16-17 - All scripture [is] given by inspiration of God, and [is] profitable for doctrine, for reproof, for correction, for instruction in righteousness:

Matthew 4:4 - But he answered and said, It is written, Man shall not live by bread alone, but by every word that proceedeth out of the mouth of God.

Ephesians 6:17 - And take the helmet of salvation, and the sword of the Spirit, which is the word of God:

Appendix B:
The Anointing and Power of Prayer

God has given us a powerful weapon that goes deeper than the comprehension of our enemy. Prayer is dialogue between man and God. When Christians pray, lives are changed, delivered, healed and set free. Prayer goes into the very deepest part of man's heart and uproots everything that should not be there.

Prayer is so powerful, and prayer's essential component is the Word of God. The Word of God captures the heart and attention of God. God responds to His Word; therefore, when Christians pray the Word and Will of God things begin to happen.

Somehow situations and circumstances conform to the will of God in the lives of believers just by praying to the powerful and sovereign God and using the only thing that God is bound by, His Word. God is bound by the Word because He is the Word, and when He couldn't find anyone or anything else to swear by His Word is his binding partner.

When I started my Christian journey, my prayer life was very minimal. But as life went on my prayer life developed more. Life situations and circumstances causes an individual to search deeper in God and to search for a hope that only God can give.

Prayer is a believer's communication tool with God. Prayer is a dialogue, not monologue. The most important person speaking is always God. He knows your situation and has the solution to any situation or problem; therefore, make sure you are listening to the voice of God when you make your petitions known to him. Prayer manifests the will of God for your life when it is applied appropriately. Prayer helps you to see yourself, first.

Below are a few scriptures concerning the power of prayer and the benefits of prayer:

John 15:7 If ye abide in me, and my words abide in you, ye shall ask what ye will, and it shall be done unto you.

Philippians 4:6 - Be careful for nothing; but in everything by prayer and supplication with thanksgiving let your requests be made known unto God.

Mark 11:24 - Therefore I say unto you, What things so ever ye desire, when ye pray, believe that ye receive [them], and ye shall have [them].

1 Thessalonians 5:17 - Pray without ceasing.

Matthew 6:7 - But when ye pray, use not vain repetitions, as the heathen [do]: for they think that they shall be heard for their much speaking.

Luke 11:9 - And I say unto you, Ask, and it shall be given you; seek, and ye shall find; knock, and it shall be opened unto you.

Romans 8:26 - Likewise the Spirit also helpeth our infirmities: for we know not what we should pray for as we ought: but the Spirit itself maketh intercession for us with groanings which cannot be uttered.

Matthew 6:6 - But thou, when thou prayest, enter into thy closet, and when thou hast shut thy door, pray to thy Father which is in secret; and thy Father which seeth in secret shall reward thee openly.

1 Timothy 2:1-4 - I exhort therefore, that, first of all, supplications, prayers, intercessions, [and] giving of thanks, be made for all men

Matthew 26:41 - Watch and pray, that ye enter not into temptation: the spirit indeed [is] willing, but the flesh [is] weak.

APPENDIX C:

THE ANOINTING AND POWER OF FAITH

In believing God for healing, deliverance and breakthroughs, it is critical that you have faith and believe that God is who He is, and Jesus Christ has already declared victory over your situation over 2,000 years ago when He was beaten, suffered, died and then resurrected by the Power of God at Calvary.

Below are powerful scriptures about faith and the anointing and power of living by faith in every aspect of your life.

Romans 10:17 - So then faith [cometh] by hearing, and hearing by the word of God.

James 2:19 - Thou believest that there is one God; thou doest well: the devils also believe, and tremble.

Hebrews 11:6 - But without faith [it is] impossible to please [him]: for he that cometh to God must believe that he is, and [that] he is a rewarder of them that diligently seek him.

Matthew 21:22 - And all things, whatsoever ye shall ask in prayer, believing, ye shall receive.

Mark 11:22-24 - And Jesus answering saith unto them, Have faith in God.

Ephesians 2:8-9 - For by grace are ye saved through faith; and that not of yourselves: [it is] the gift of God:

Luke 1:37 - For with God nothing shall be impossible.

Hebrews 11:1 - Now faith is the substance of things hoped for, the evidence of things not seen.

Hebrews 11:1 - 13:25 - Now faith is the substance of things hoped for, the evidence of things not seen.

Ephesians 2:8 - For by grace are ye saved through faith; and that not of yourselves: [it is] the gift of God:

Corinthians 2:5 - That your faith should not stand in the wisdom of men, but in the power of God.

Proverbs 3:5-6 - Trust in the LORD with all thine heart; and lean not unto thine own understanding.

James 2:24 - Ye see then how that by works a man is justified, and not by faith only.

James 2:14-26 - What [doth it] profit, my brethren, though a man say he hath faith, and have not works? can faith save him?

Corinthians 5:7 - (For we walk by faith, not by sight:)

Psalms 46:10 - Be still, and know that I [am] God: I will be exalted among the heathen, I will be exalted in the earth.

Appendix D:

The Anointing and Power in Healing

Throughout the Bible, healings are notated. Jesus healed all manner of diseases and afflictions. Jesus sometimes spoke the Word and people were healed, He touched some and had compassion for others that manifest life-changing situations in the lives of many. It is the will of God that His people be healed and set free. The Word of God expresses this Will so profoundly. Below are scriptures to help increase your faith that healing will manifest in every situation and circumstance in life.

Jeremiah 17:14 - Heal me, O LORD, and I shall be healed; save me, and I shall be saved: for thou [art] my praise.

1 Peter 2:24 - Who his own self bare our sins in his own body on the tree, that we, being dead to sins, should live unto righteousness: by whose stripes ye were healed.

Jeremiah 33:6 - Behold, I will bring it health and cure, and I will cure them, and will reveal unto them the abundance of peace and truth.

Isaiah 53:5 - But he [was] wounded for our transgressions, [he was] bruised for our iniquities: the chastisement of our peace [was] upon him; and with his stripes we are healed.

Psalms 103:2-4 - Bless the LORD, O my soul, and forget not all his benefits:

James 5:15 - And the prayer of faith shall save the sick, and the Lord shall raise him up; and if he has committed sins, they shall be forgiven him.

James 5:14 - Is any sick among you? let him call for the elders of the church; and let them pray over him, anointing him with oil in the name of the Lord:

James 5:16 - Confess [your] faults one to another, and pray one for another, that ye may be healed. The effectual fervent prayer of a righteous man availeth much.

3 John 1:2 - Beloved, I wish above all things that thou mayest prosper and be in health, even as thy soul prospereth.

Matthew 10:1 - And when he had called unto [him] his twelve disciples, he gave them power [against] unclean spirits, to cast them out, and to heal all manner of sickness and all manner of disease.

Matthew 10:8 - Heal the sick, cleanse the lepers, raise the dead, cast out devils: freely ye have received, freely give.

Deuteronomy 7:15 - And the LORD will take away from thee all sickness, and will put none of the evil diseases of Egypt, which thou knowest, upon thee; but will lay them upon all [them] that hate thee.

www.ingramcontent.com/pod-product-compliance
Lightning Source LLC
Chambersburg PA
CBHW051712090426
42736CB00013B/2672